DRAWING 100 Fun & Easy CHRISTMAS ITEMS

The Good and the Beautiful

INSTRUCTIONS

MATERIALS NEEDED:

- Standard #2 pencil, sharpened
- Kneaded eraser
- Sketch paper

INSTRUCTIONS:

Draw a large square on your sketch paper. This will help you scale your image appropriately. Then, draw the images as shown in each step, taking care to press your pencil lightly on the paper as you will need to erase certain elements as you progress through the steps of the project.

1

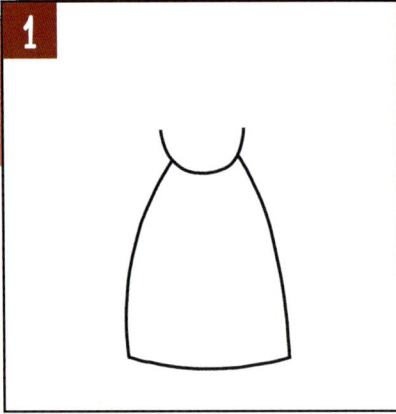

2

3

1
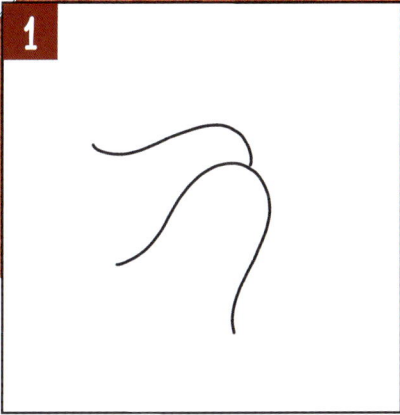

2

3

4

4

1

2

3
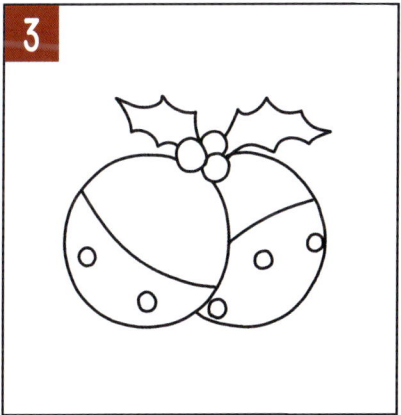

4
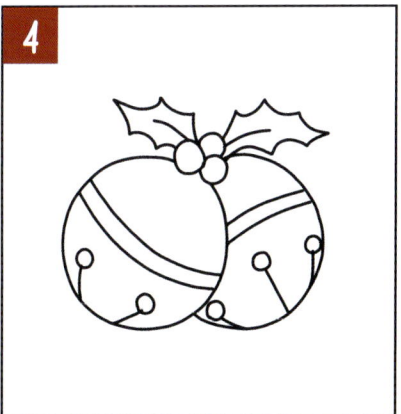

1

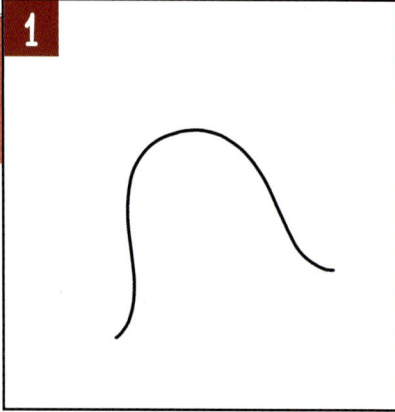

2

3

4

1

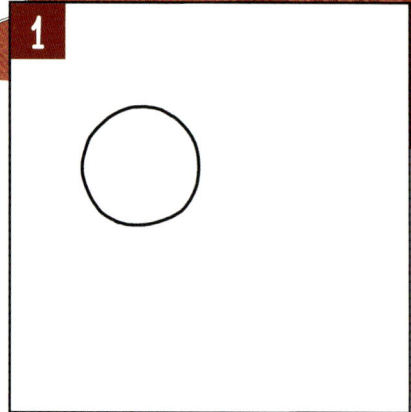

2

3

4

7

1

2

3

4

8

1
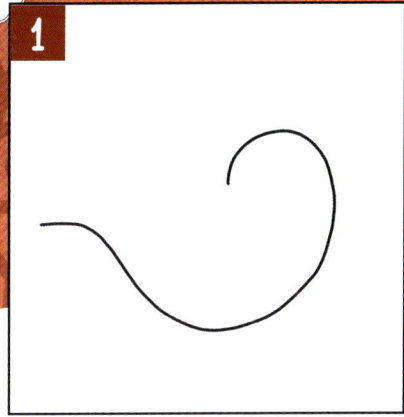

2

3

4

1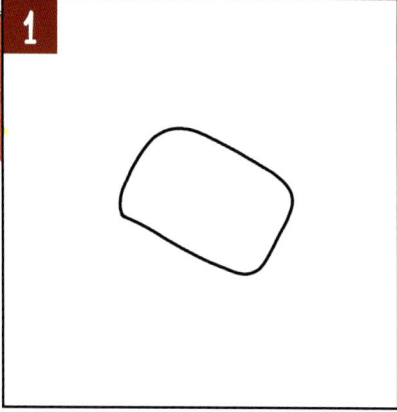

1

2

2

3

3

4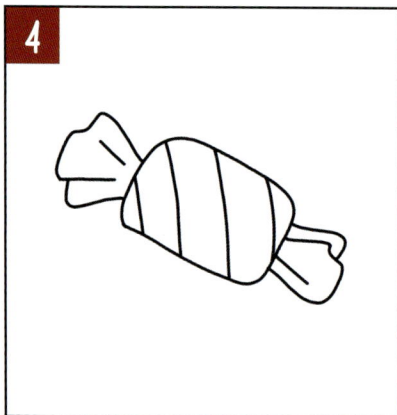

4

THE GOOD AND THE BEAUTIFUL | DRAWING 100 FUN & EASY CHRISTMAS ITEMS

1

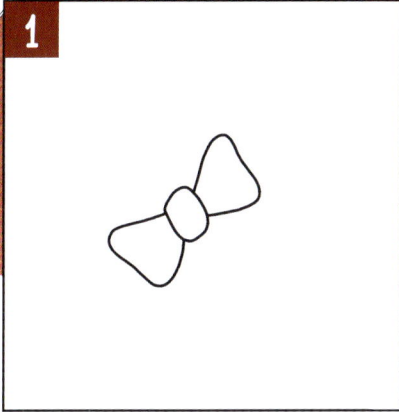

1

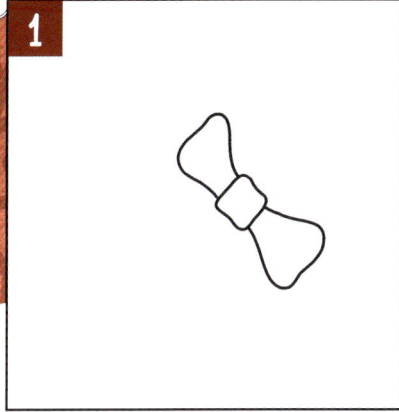

2

2

3

3

4

4

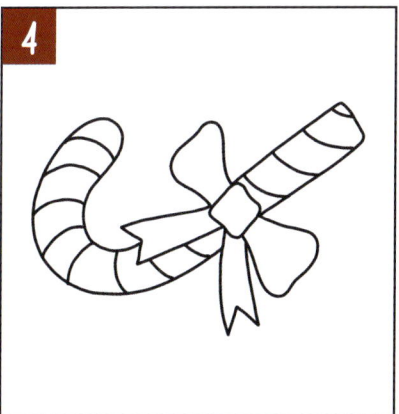

THE GOOD AND THE BEAUTIFUL | DRAWING 100 FUN & EASY CHRISTMAS ITEMS

1

1

2

2

3

3

4

4

THE GOOD AND THE BEAUTIFUL | DRAWING 100 FUN & EASY CHRISTMAS ITEMS

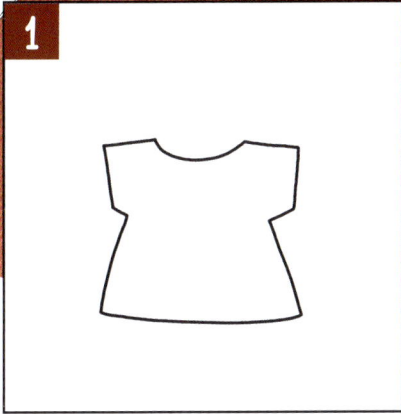

THE GOOD AND THE BEAUTIFUL | DRAWING 100 FUN & EASY CHRISTMAS ITEMS

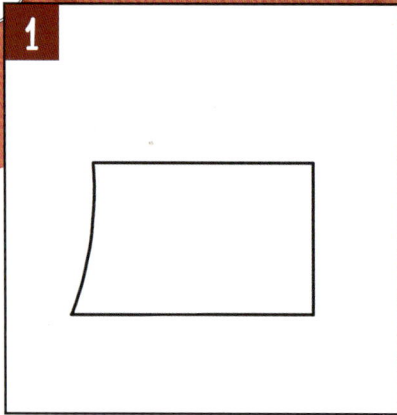

THE GOOD AND THE BEAUTIFUL | DRAWING 100 FUN & EASY CHRISTMAS ITEMS

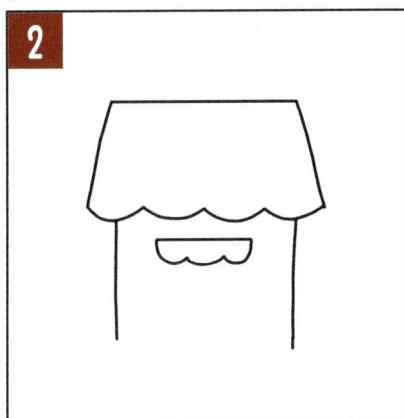

1

2

3

4

1

2

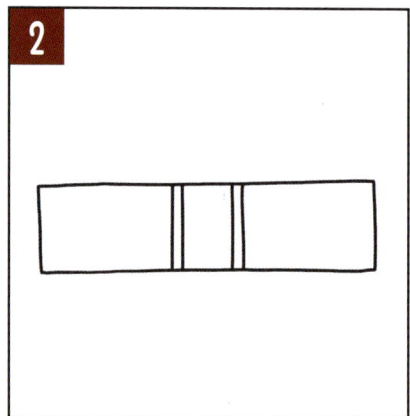

3

4

THE GOOD AND THE BEAUTIFUL | DRAWING 100 FUN & EASY CHRISTMAS ITEMS

23

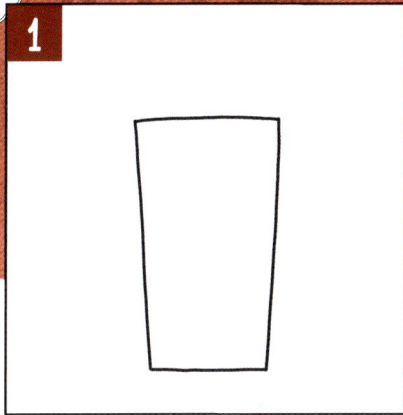

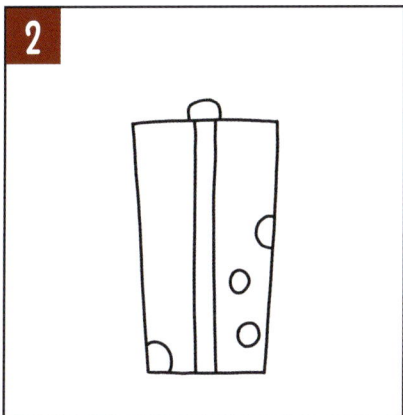

24

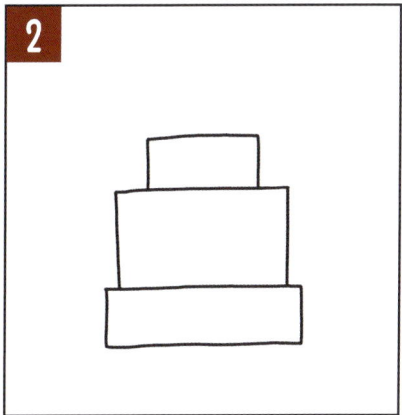

1

2

3

4

1

2

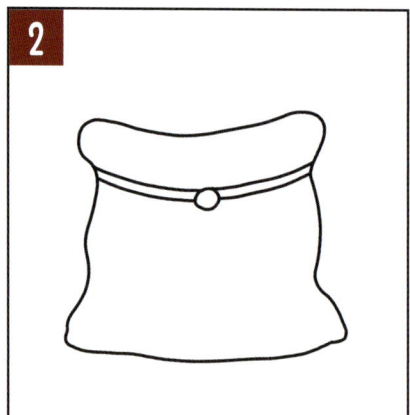

3

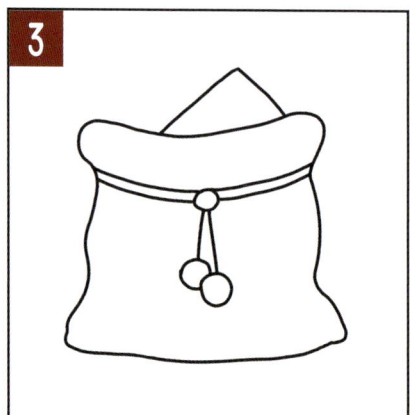

4

THE GOOD AND THE BEAUTIFUL | DRAWING 100 FUN & EASY CHRISTMAS ITEMS

27

1
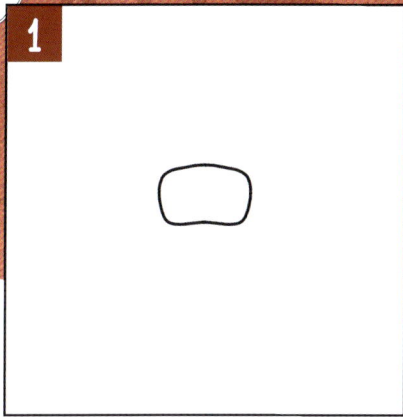

2

3

4

28

1
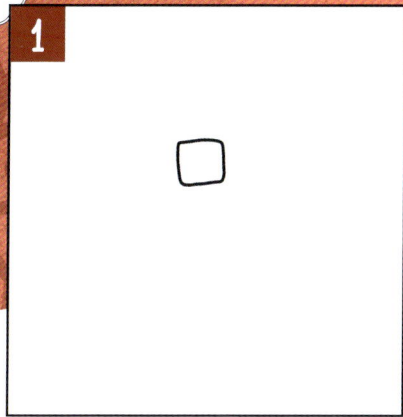

2

3

4

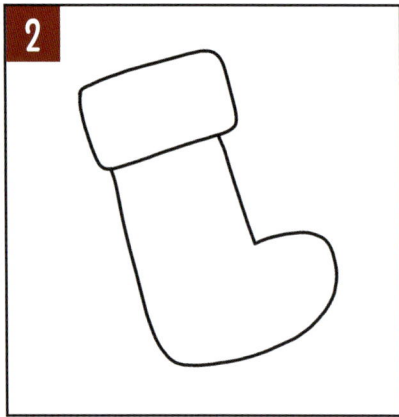

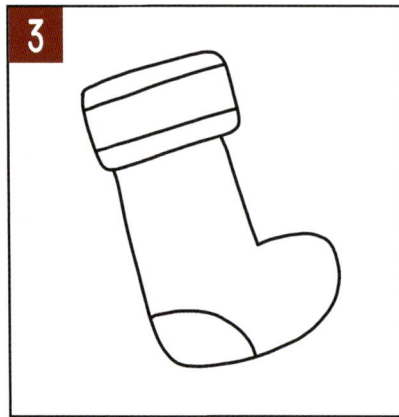

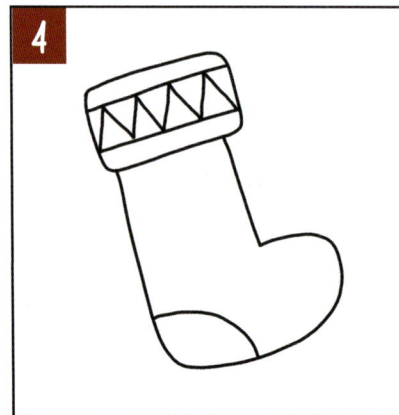

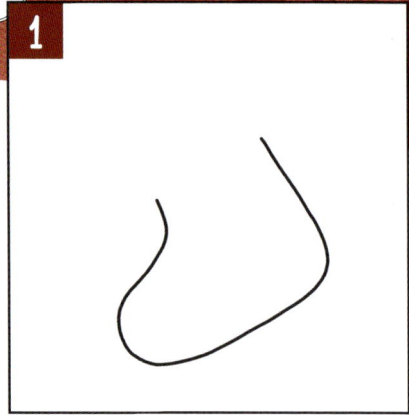

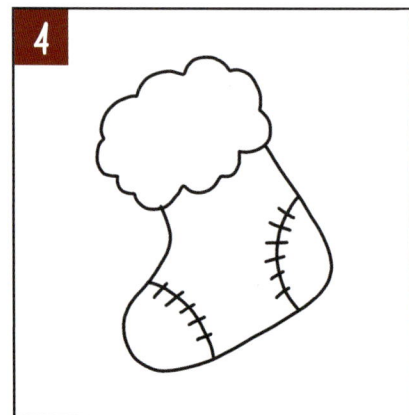

THE GOOD AND THE BEAUTIFUL | DRAWING 100 FUN & EASY CHRISTMAS ITEMS

1

1

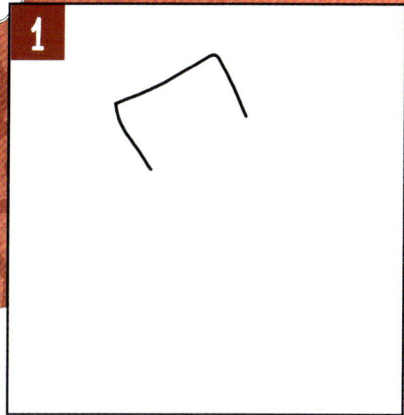

2

2

3

3

4

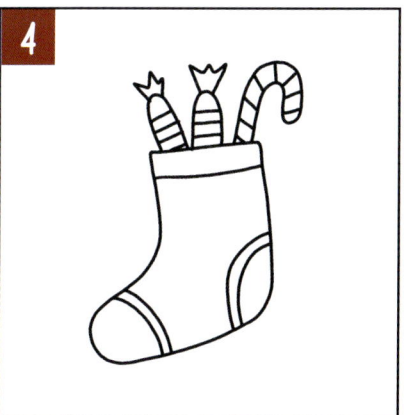

4

THE GOOD AND THE BEAUTIFUL | DRAWING 100 FUN & EASY CHRISTMAS ITEMS

1

1

2

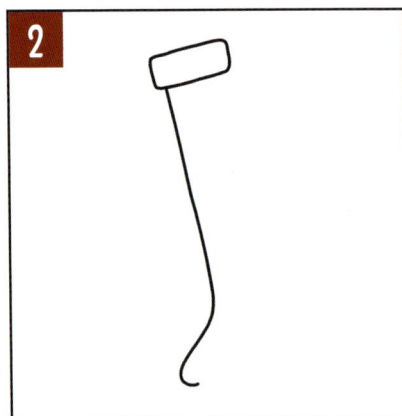

2

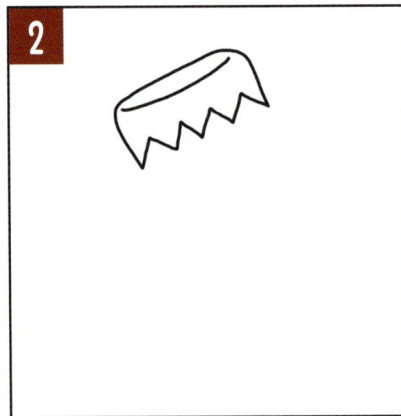

3

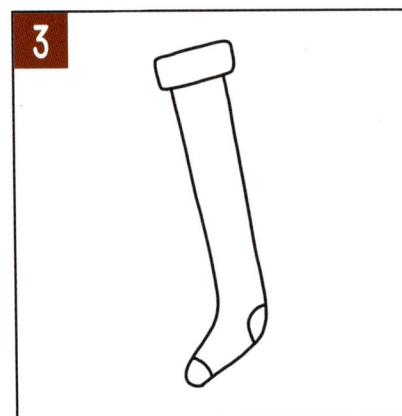

3

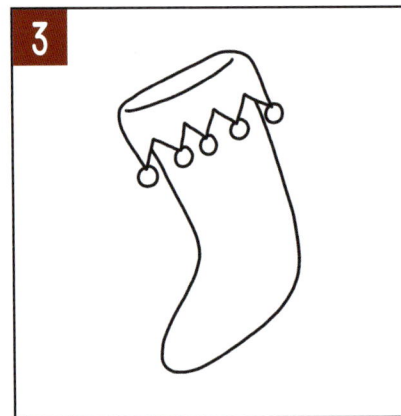

4

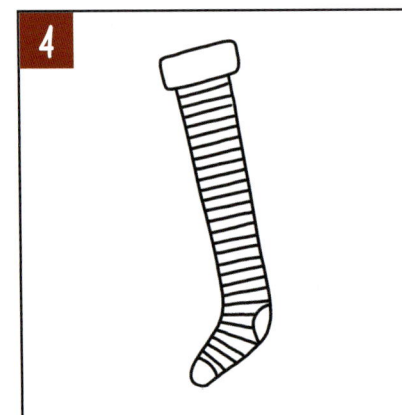

4

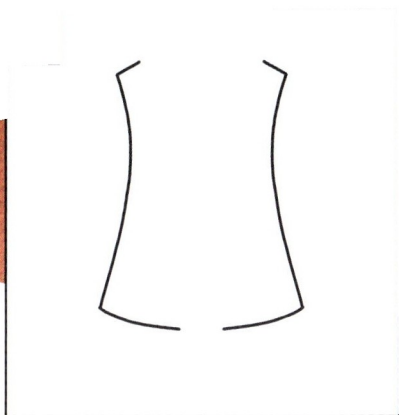

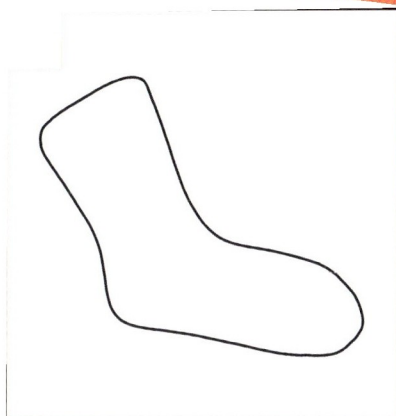

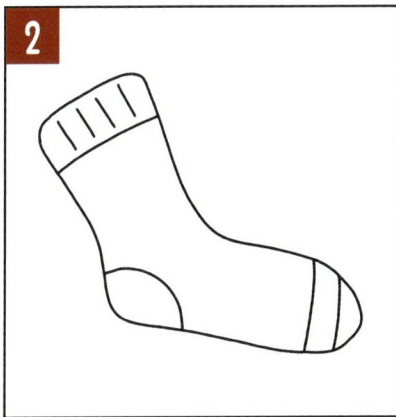

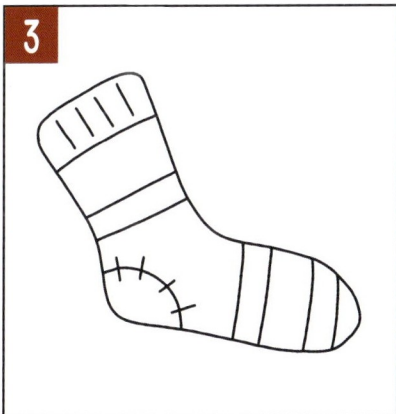

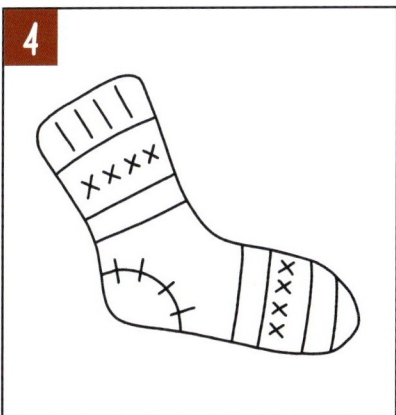

1

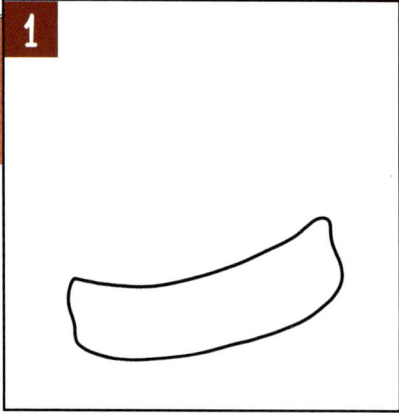

1

2

2

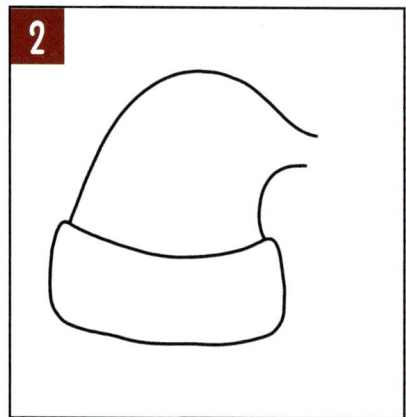

3

3

4

4

THE GOOD AND THE BEAUTIFUL | DRAWING 100 FUN & EASY CHRISTMAS ITEMS

1

2

3

4

1

2

3

4

THE GOOD AND THE BEAUTIFUL | DRAWING 100 FUN & EASY CHRISTMAS ITEMS

1
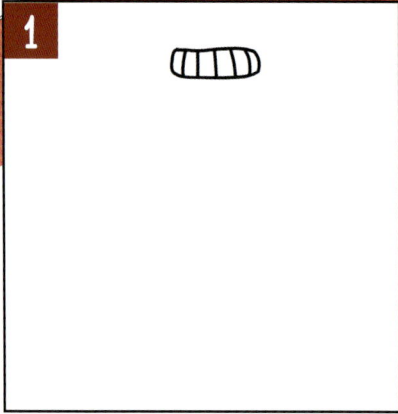

1

2

2

3

3
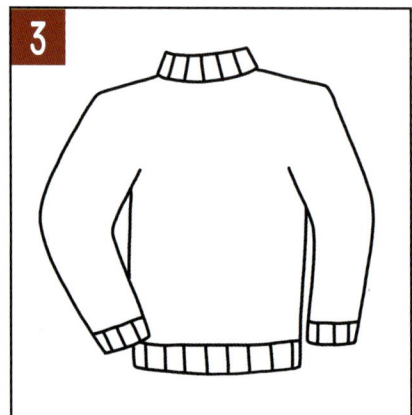

4

4

THE GOOD AND THE BEAUTIFUL | DRAWING 100 FUN & EASY CHRISTMAS ITEMS

43

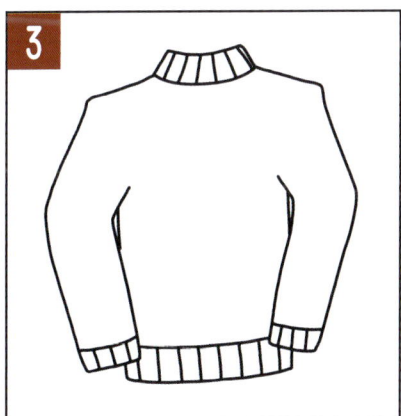

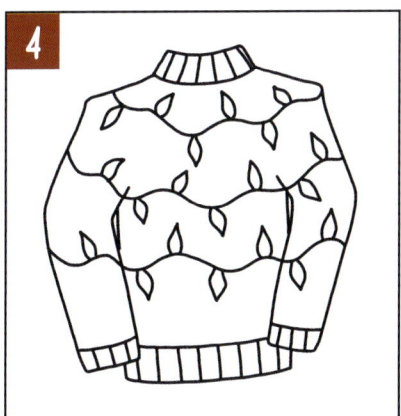

44

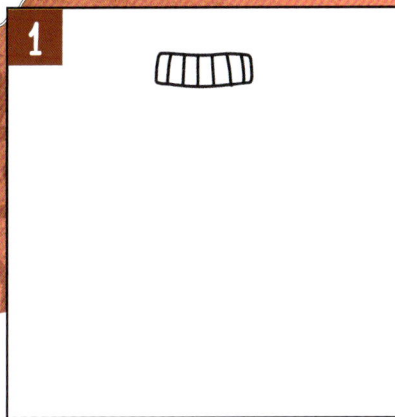

1

1

2

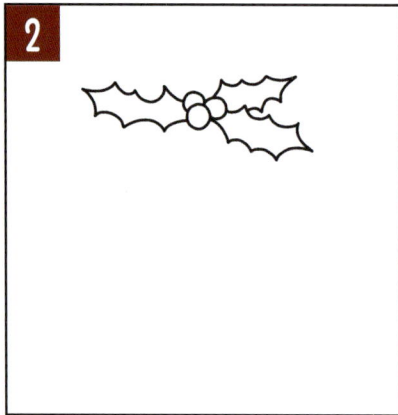

2

3

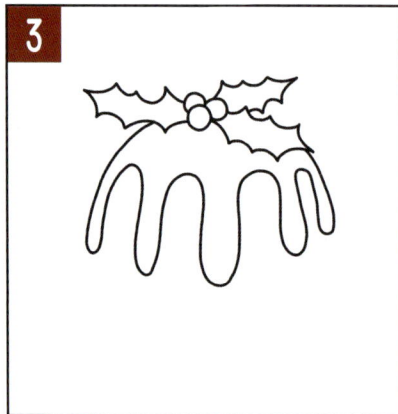

3

4

4

47

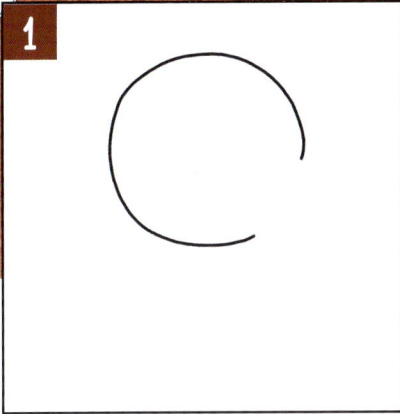

48

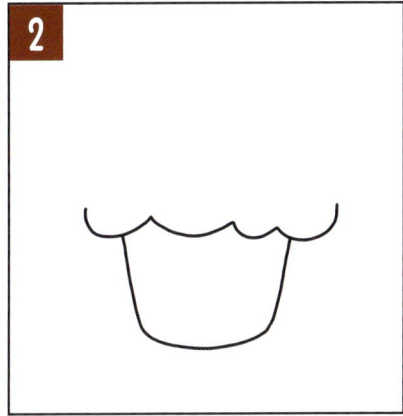

THE GOOD AND THE BEAUTIFUL | DRAWING 100 FUN & EASY CHRISTMAS ITEMS

1

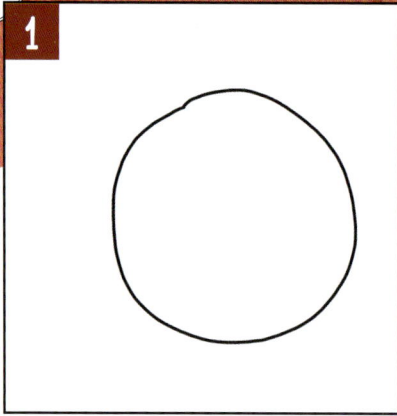

1

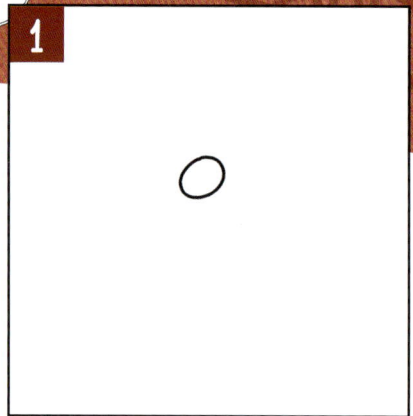

2

2

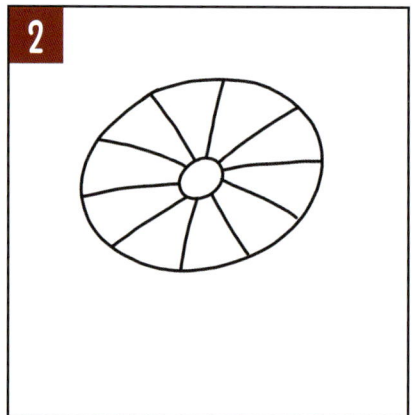

3

3

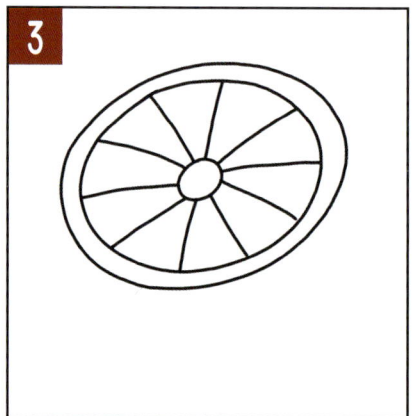

4

4

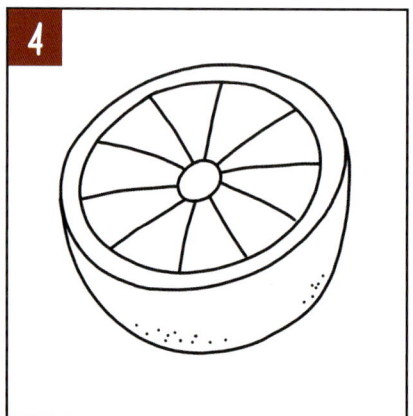

THE GOOD AND THE BEAUTIFUL | DRAWING 100 FUN & EASY CHRISTMAS ITEMS

1

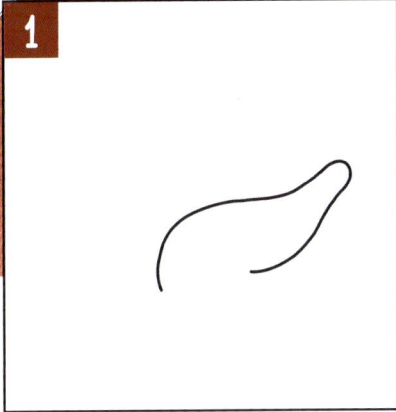

2

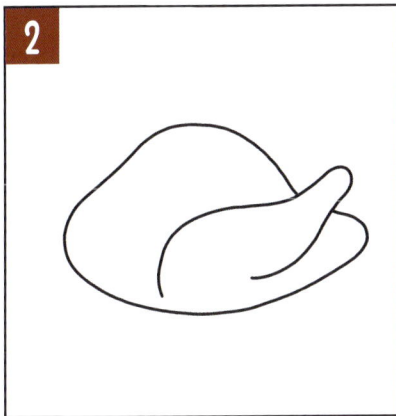

3

4

1

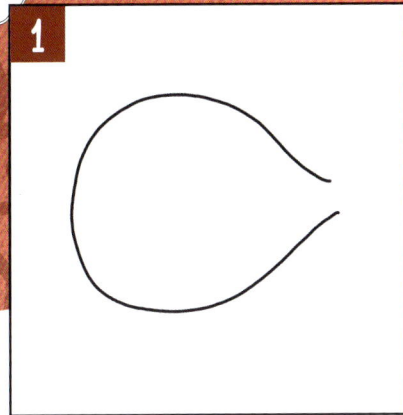

2

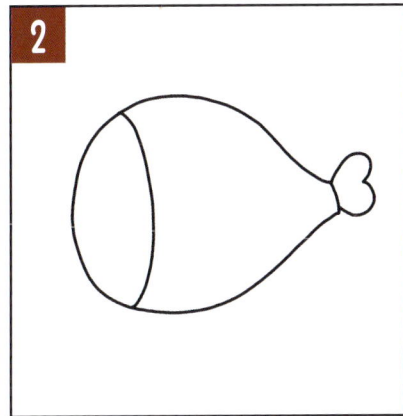

3

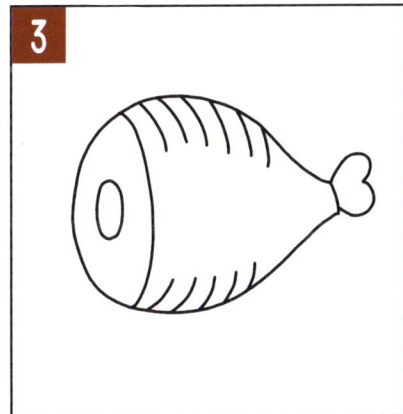

4

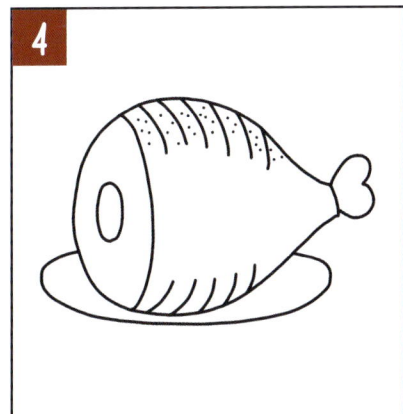

THE GOOD AND THE BEAUTIFUL | DRAWING 100 FUN & EASY CHRISTMAS ITEMS

1

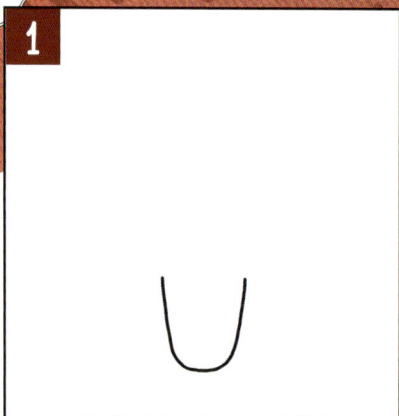

2

3

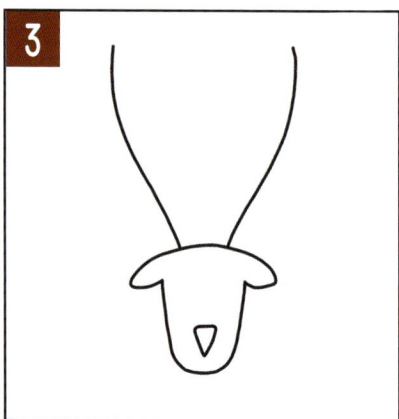

4

1

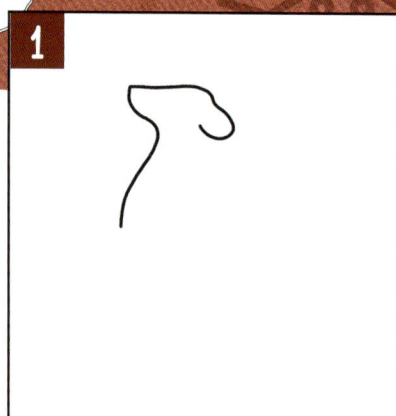

2

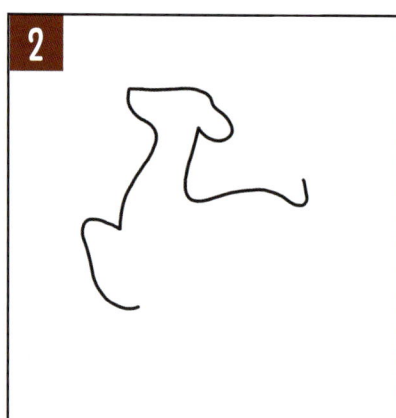

3

4

THE GOOD AND THE BEAUTIFUL | DRAWING 100 FUN & EASY CHRISTMAS ITEMS

55

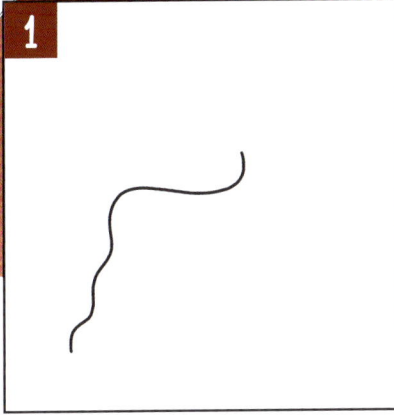

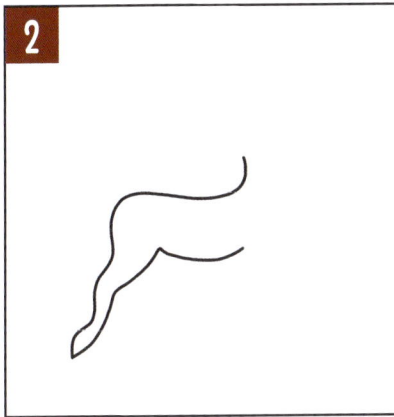

56

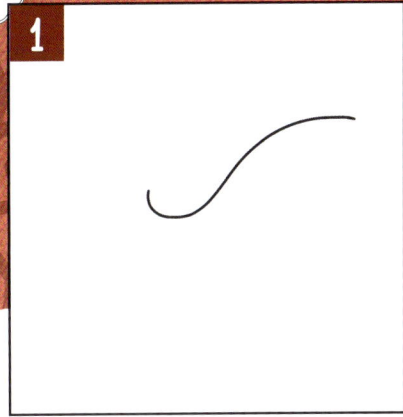

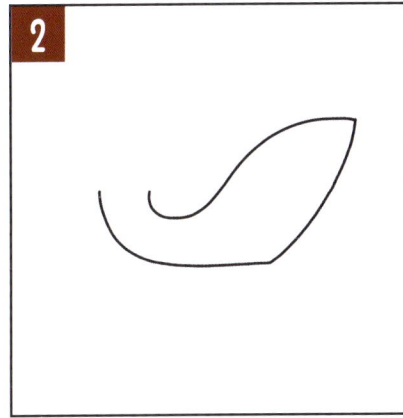

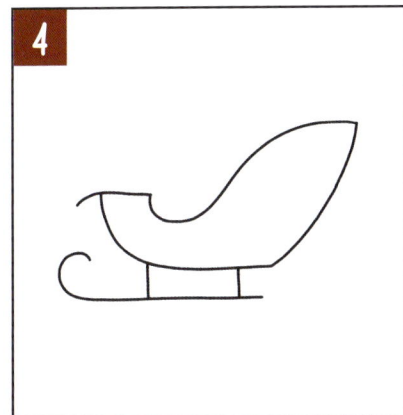

1

2

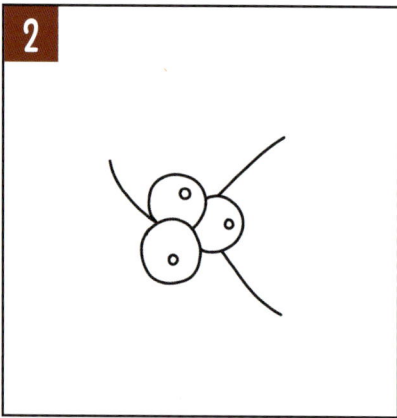

3

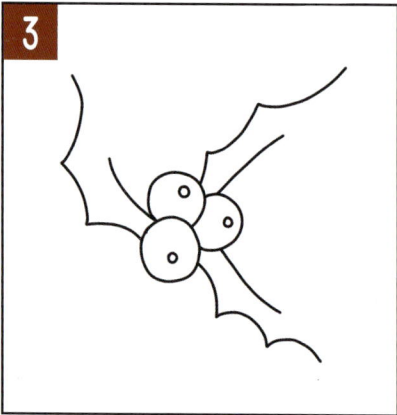

4

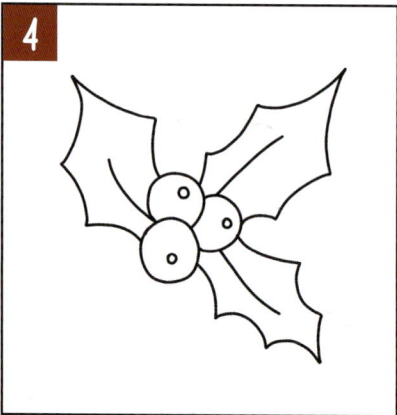

1

2

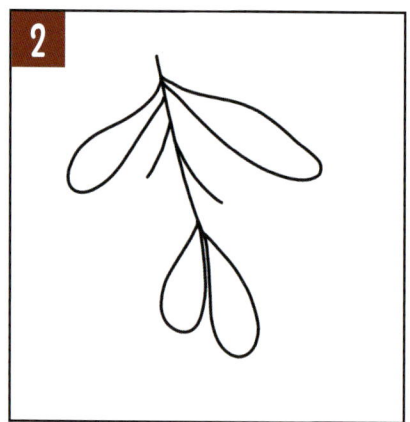

3

4

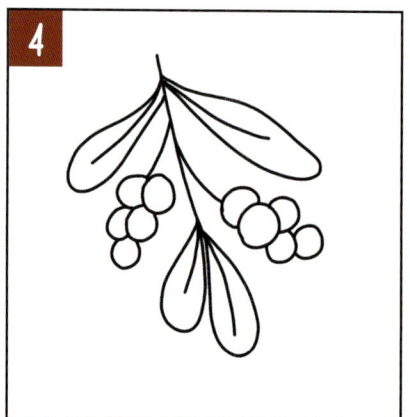

THE GOOD AND THE BEAUTIFUL | DRAWING 100 FUN & EASY CHRISTMAS ITEMS

1

2

3

4

1

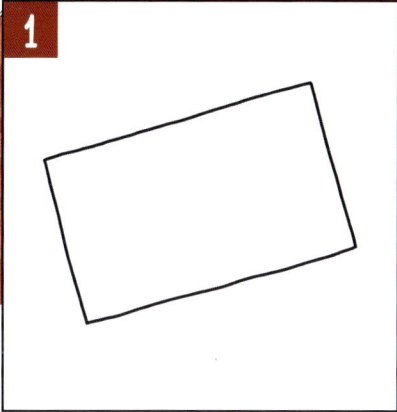

2

3

4

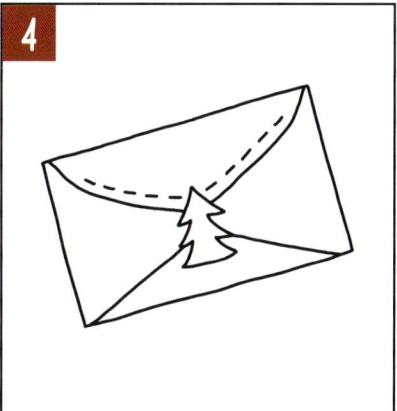

1

1

2

2

3

3

4

4

THE GOOD AND THE BEAUTIFUL | DRAWING 100 FUN & EASY CHRISTMAS ITEMS

1

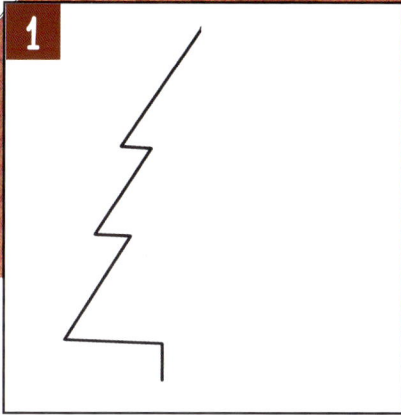

2

3

4

1

2

3

4

THE GOOD AND THE BEAUTIFUL | DRAWING 100 FUN & EASY CHRISTMAS ITEMS

1

1

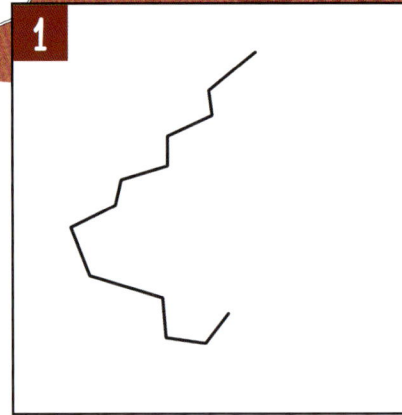

2

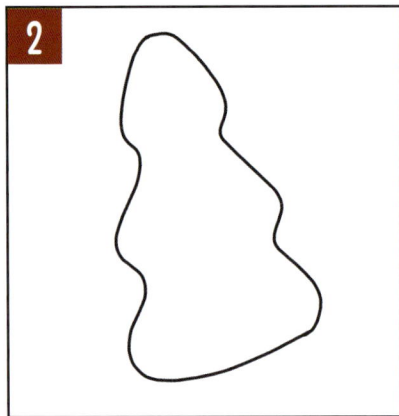

2

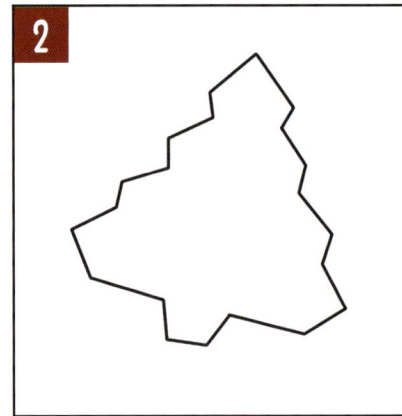

3

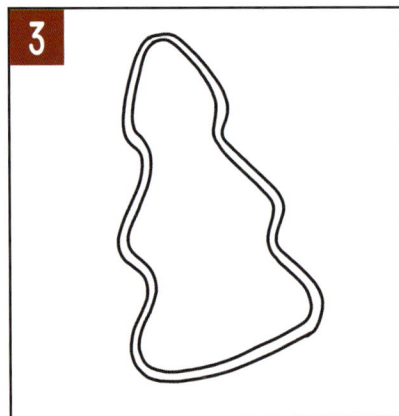

3

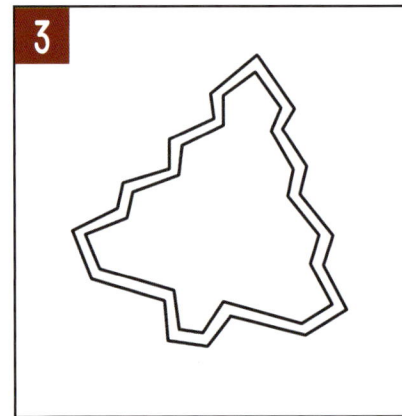

4

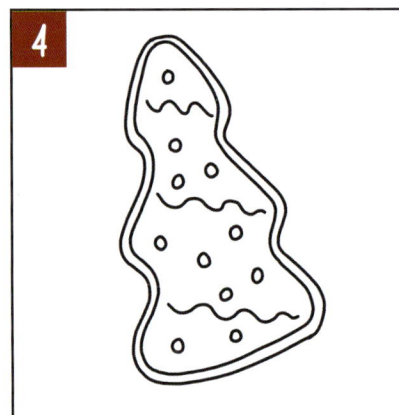

4

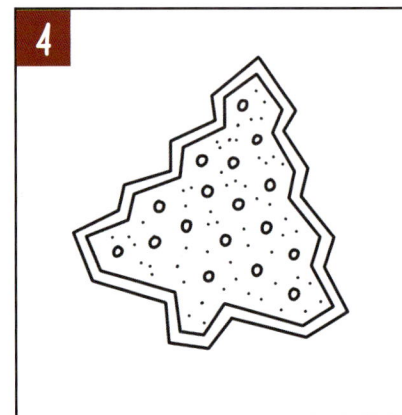

THE GOOD AND THE BEAUTIFUL | DRAWING 100 FUN & EASY CHRISTMAS ITEMS

1

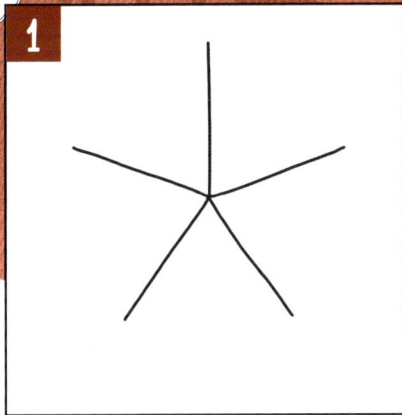

1

2

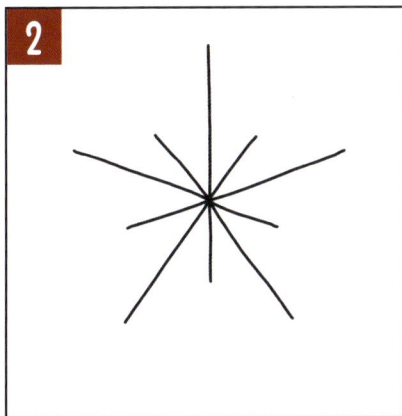

2

3

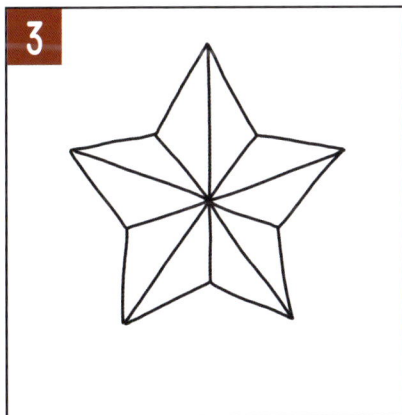

3

4

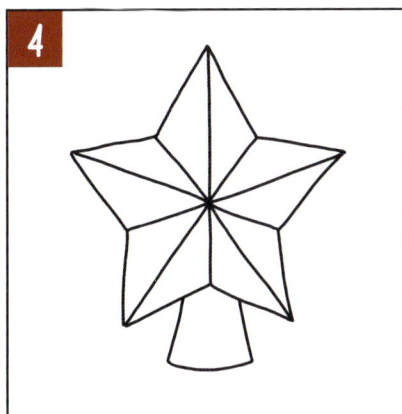

4

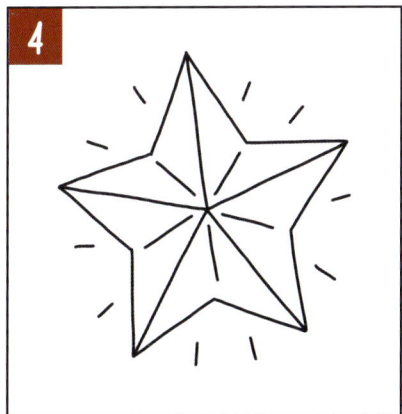

THE GOOD AND THE BEAUTIFUL | DRAWING 100 FUN & EASY CHRISTMAS ITEMS

1

2

3

4

1

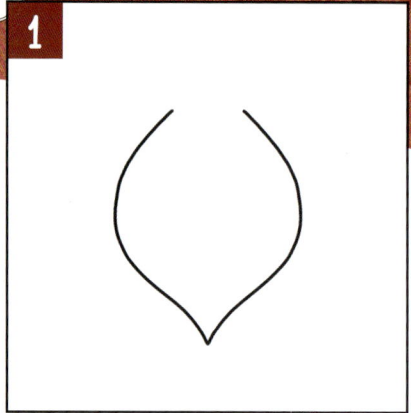

2

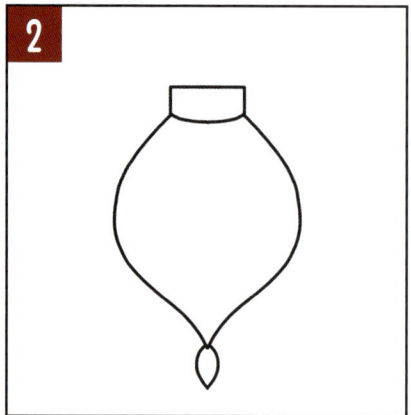

3

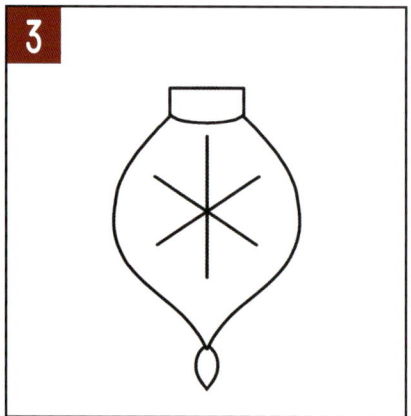

4

THE GOOD AND THE BEAUTIFUL | DRAWING 100 FUN & EASY CHRISTMAS ITEMS

1

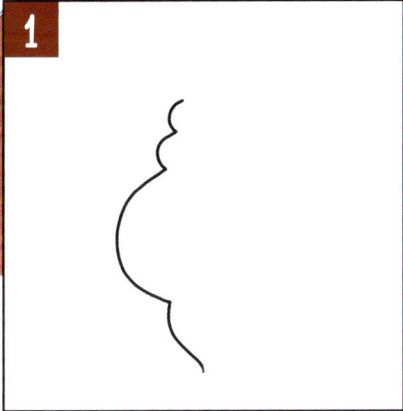

2

3

4

1

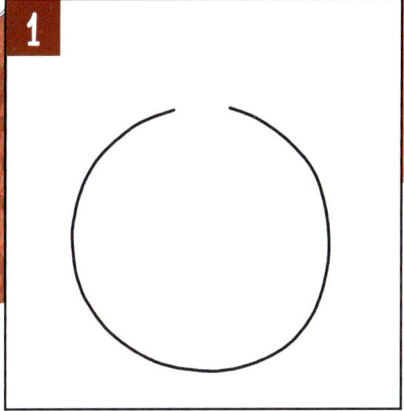

2

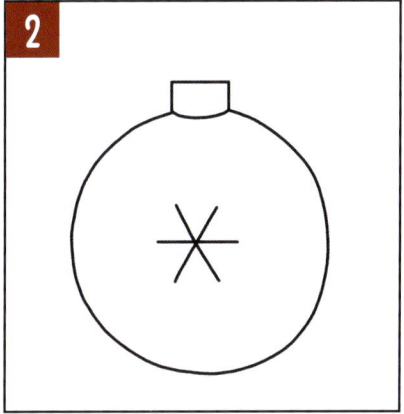

3

4

1

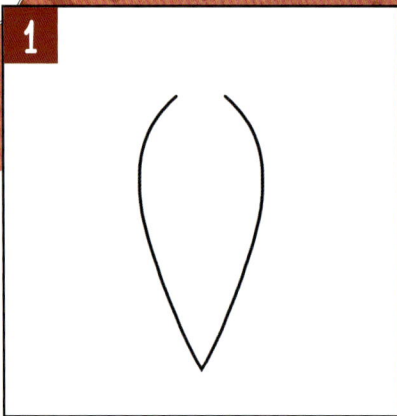

2

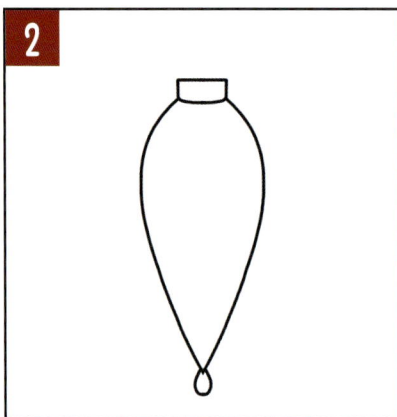

3

4

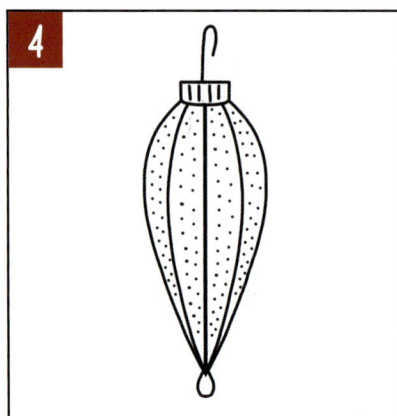

1

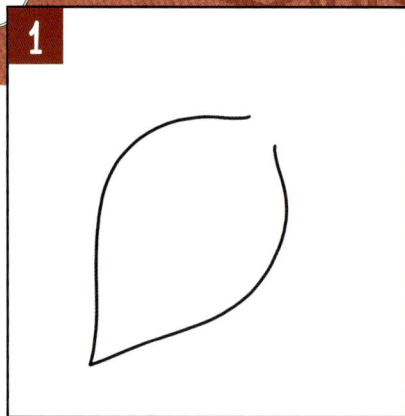

2

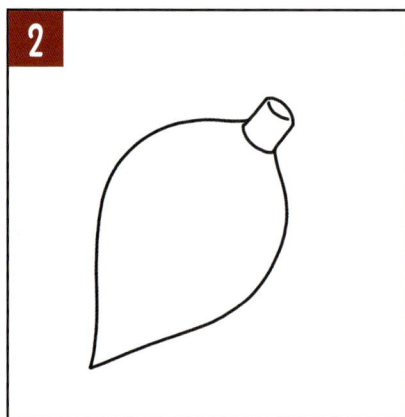

3

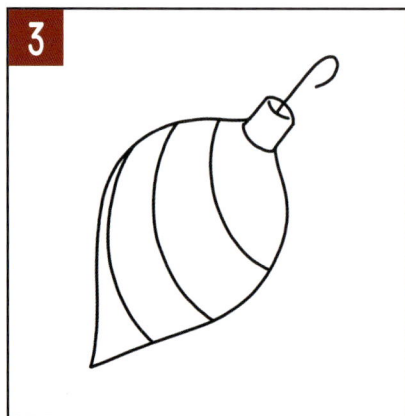

4

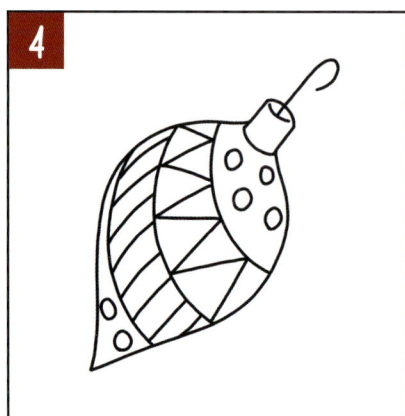

THE GOOD AND THE BEAUTIFUL | DRAWING 100 FUN & EASY CHRISTMAS ITEMS

75

1

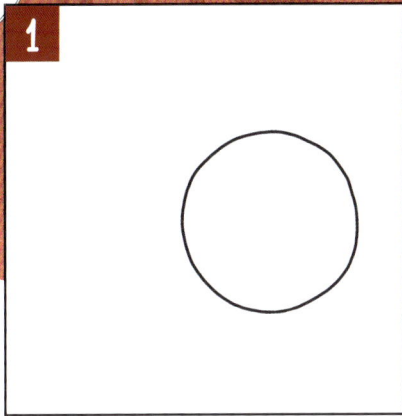

2

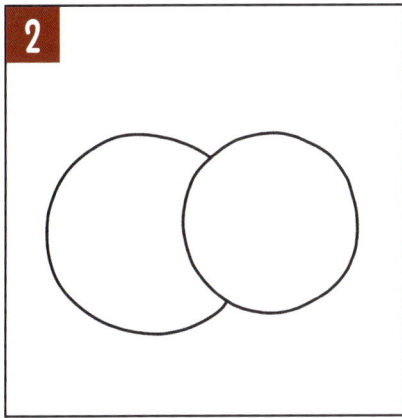

3

4

76

1

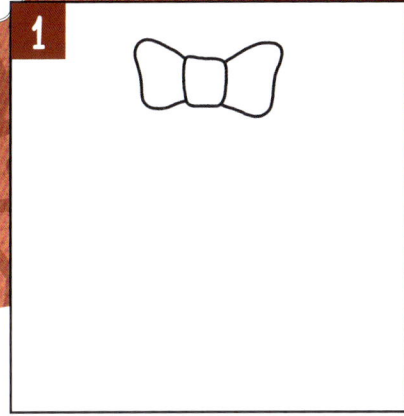

2

3

4

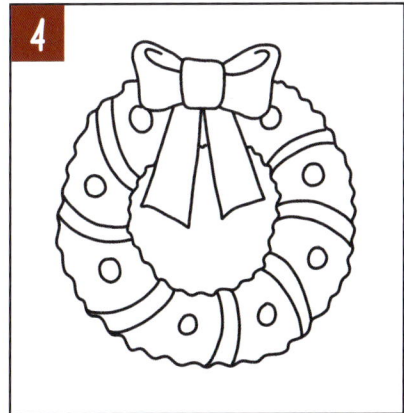

1

2

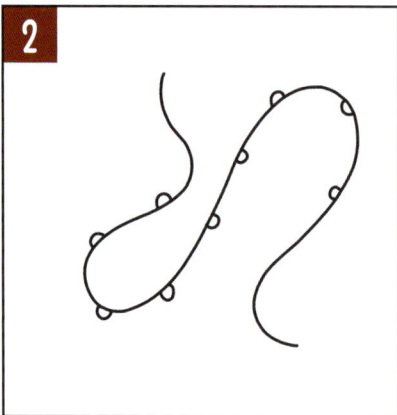

3

4

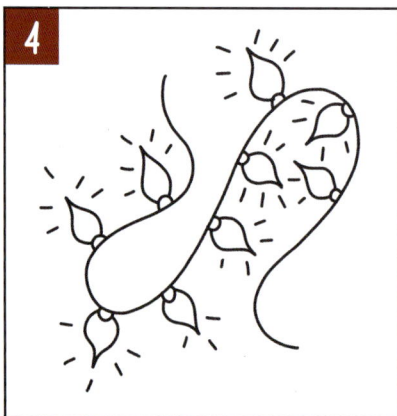

1

2

3

1

1

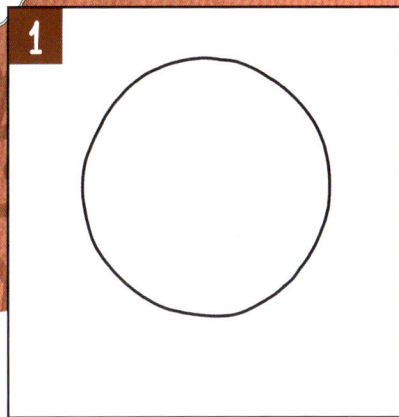

2

2

3

3

4

4

THE GOOD AND THE BEAUTIFUL | DRAWING 100 FUN & EASY CHRISTMAS ITEMS

1

2

3

4

1

2

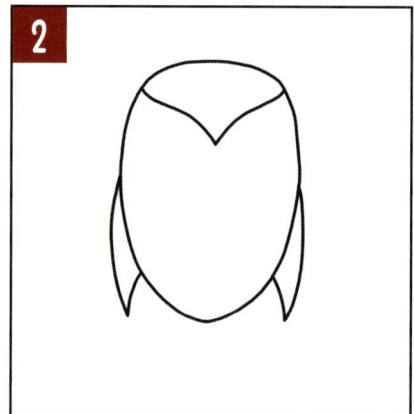

3

4

THE GOOD AND THE BEAUTIFUL | DRAWING 100 FUN & EASY CHRISTMAS ITEMS

1

1

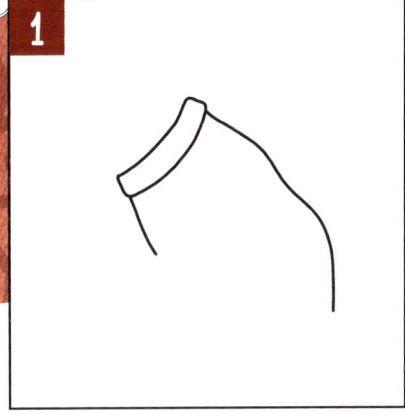

2

2

3

3

4

4

THE GOOD AND THE BEAUTIFUL | DRAWING 100 FUN & EASY CHRISTMAS ITEMS

1

2

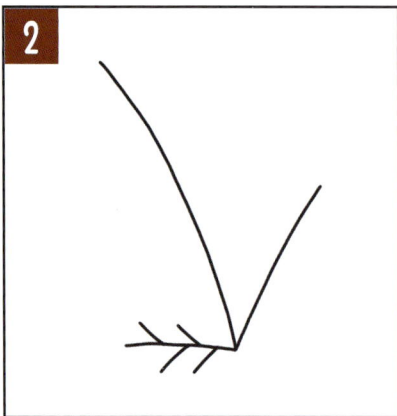

3

4

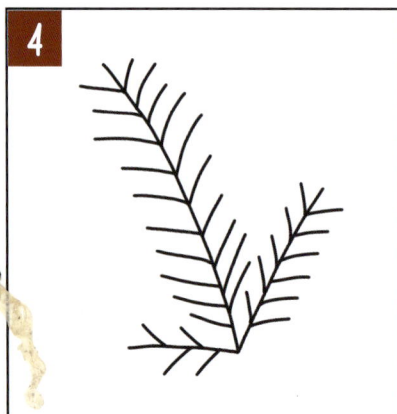

1

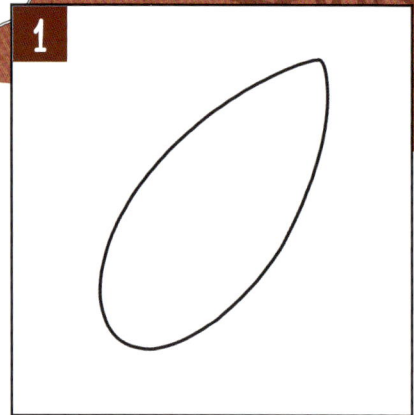

2

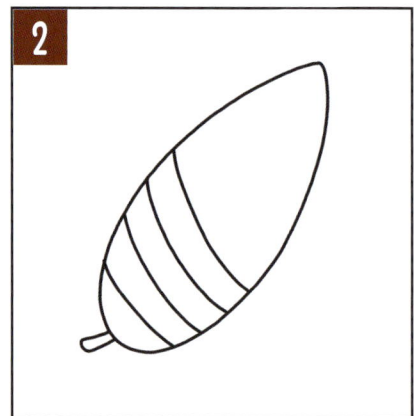

3

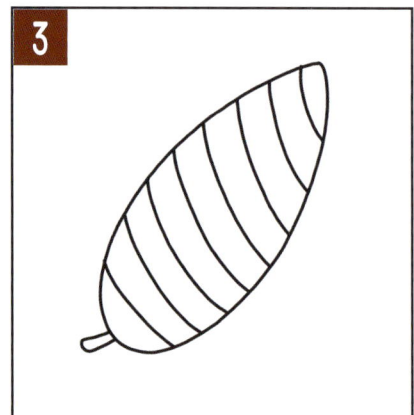

4

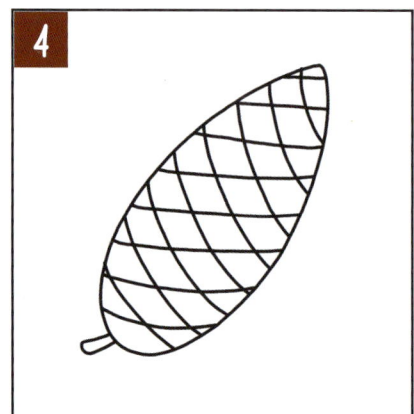

THE GOOD AND THE BEAUTIFUL | DRAWING 100 FUN & EASY CHRISTMAS ITEMS

1

1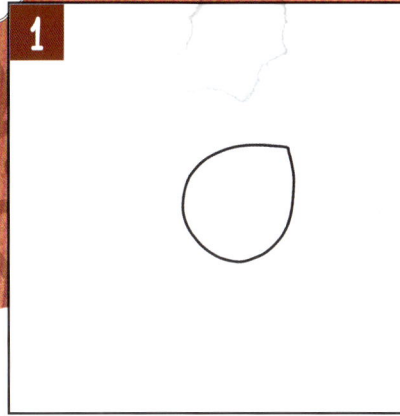

2

2

3

3

4

4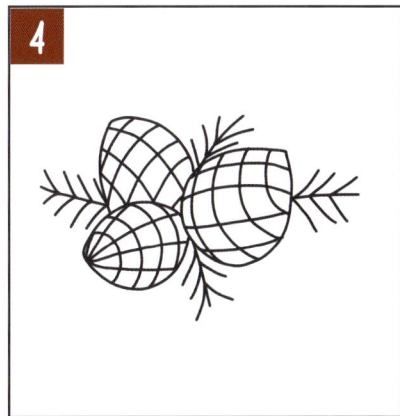

THE GOOD AND THE BEAUTIFUL | DRAWING 100 FUN & EASY CHRISTMAS ITEMS

1

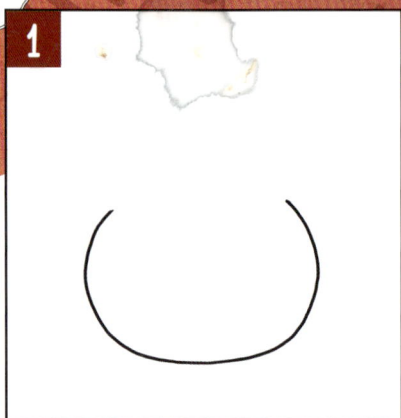

2

3

4

1

2

3

4

THE GOOD AND THE BEAUTIFUL | DRAWING 100 FUN & EASY CHRISTMAS ITEMS

91

92

93

1

2
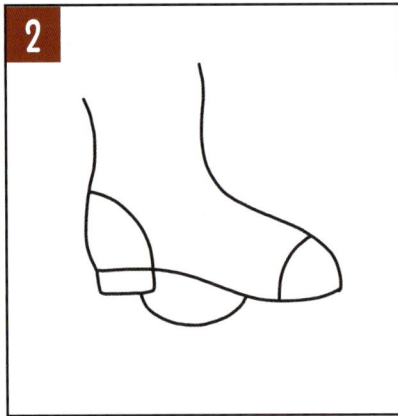

3
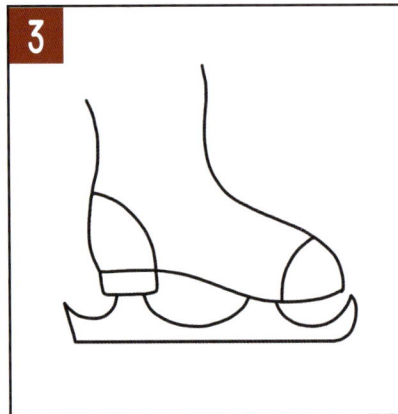

4

94

1
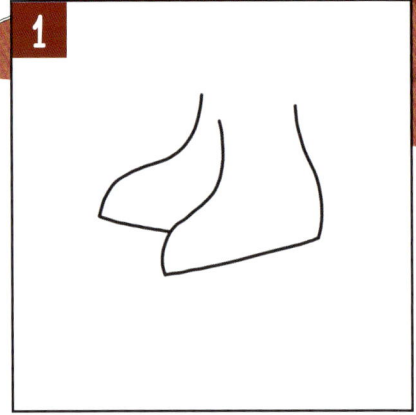

2
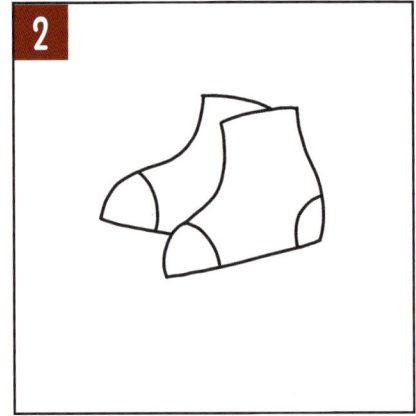

3
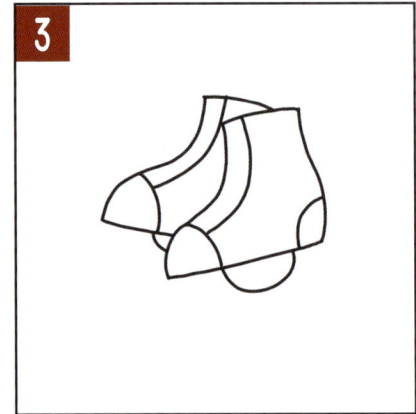

4
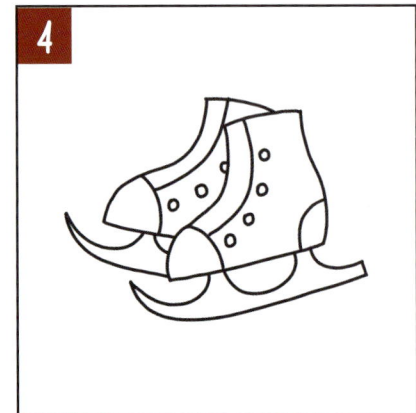

1

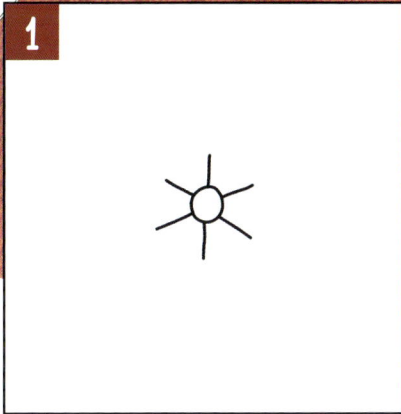

1

2

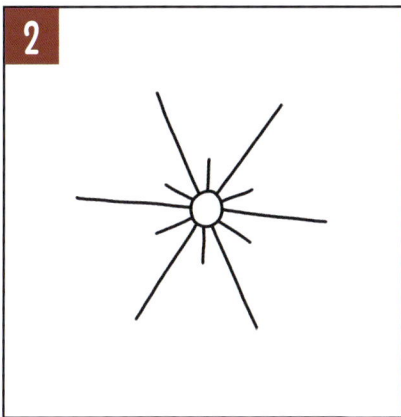

2

3

3

4

4

THE GOOD AND THE BEAUTIFUL | DRAWING 100 FUN & EASY CHRISTMAS ITEMS

1

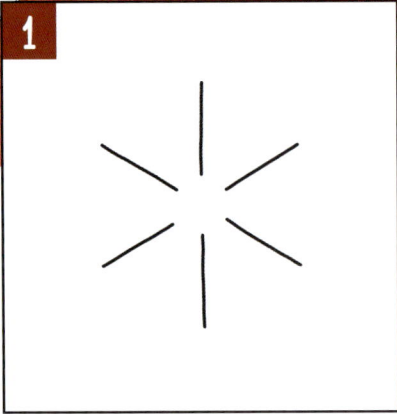

2

3

4

1

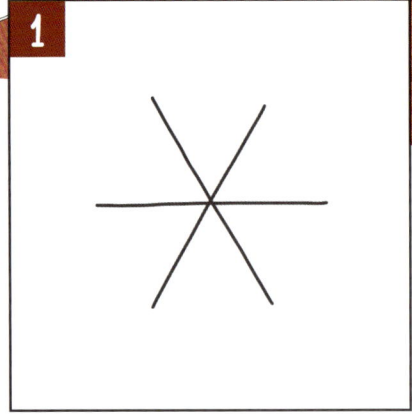

2

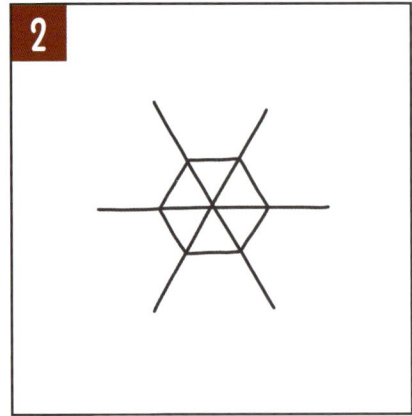

3

4

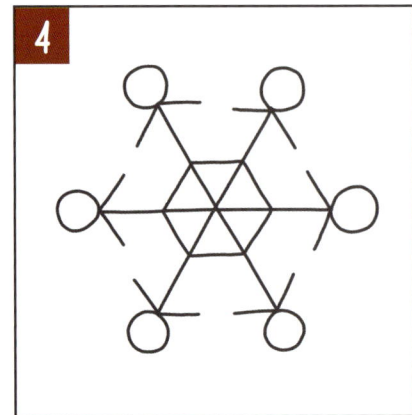

THE GOOD AND THE BEAUTIFUL | DRAWING 100 FUN & EASY CHRISTMAS ITEMS

1

1
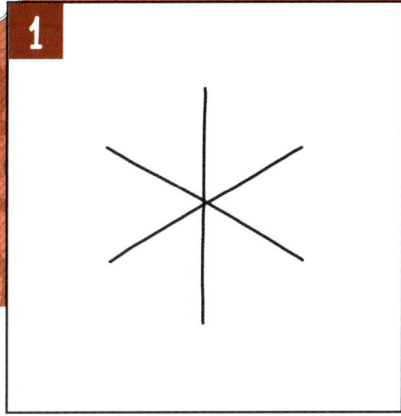

2
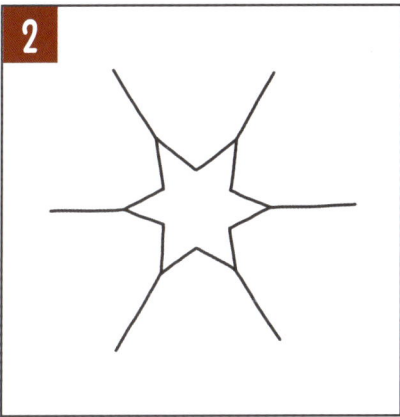

2

3
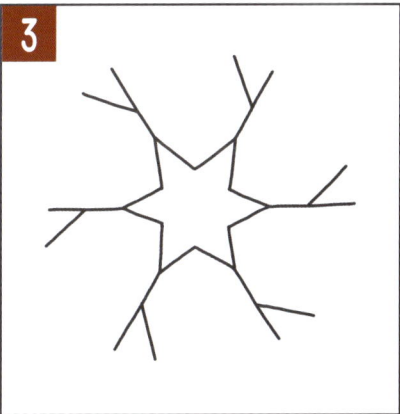

3

4
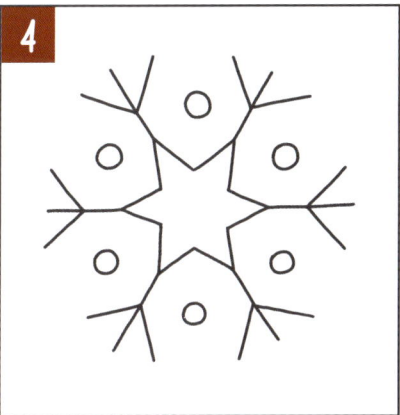

4
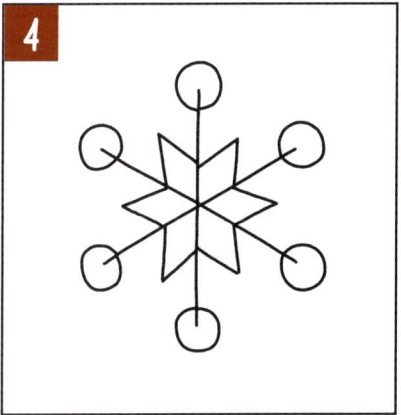

THE GOOD AND THE BEAUTIFUL | DRAWING 100 FUN & EASY CHRISTMAS ITEMS

51

COMPLETE THIS SCENE BY DRAWING YOUR FAVORITE CHRISTMAS
ITEMS ON THE TREE, ON THE HILLS, AND HANGING FROM THE STRINGS.

FREE DRAW

FREE DRAW

FREE DRAW

FREE DRAW

MORE DRAWING BOOKS FROM THE GOOD AND THE BEAUTIFUL

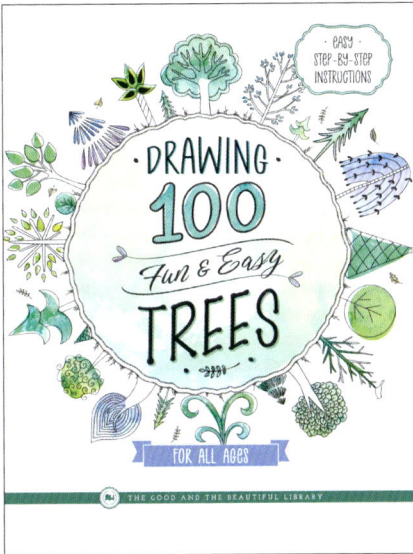

DRAWING **100** *Fun & Easy* TREES

easy step-by-step instructions

FOR ALL AGES

THE GOOD AND THE BEAUTIFUL LIBRARY

Sample from Drawing Trees

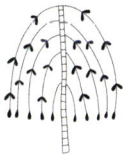

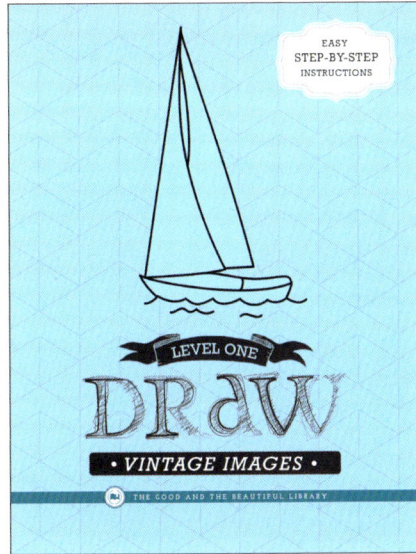

EASY STEP-BY-STEP INSTRUCTIONS

LEVEL ONE

DRAW

• VINTAGE IMAGES •

THE GOOD AND THE BEAUTIFUL LIBRARY

Sample from Level One

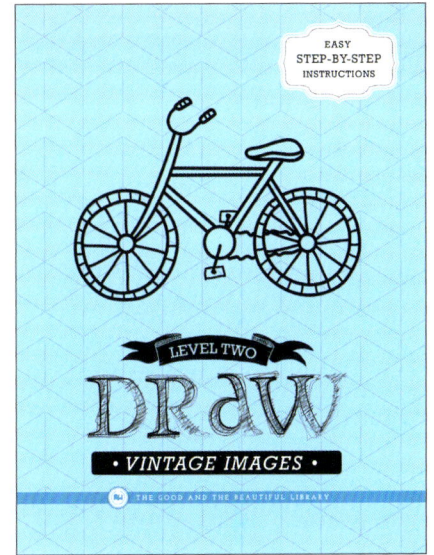

EASY STEP-BY-STEP INSTRUCTIONS

LEVEL TWO

DRAW

• VINTAGE IMAGES •

THE GOOD AND THE BEAUTIFUL LIBRARY

Sample from Level Two

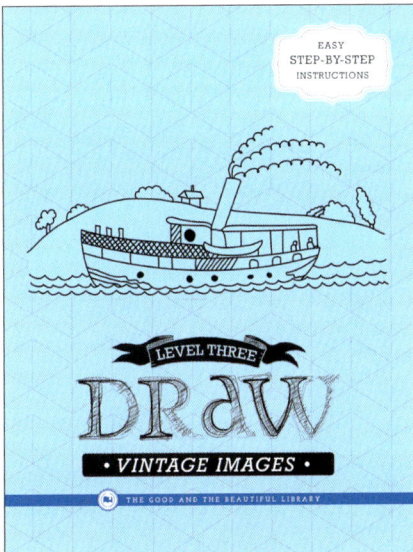

EASY STEP-BY-STEP INSTRUCTIONS

LEVEL THREE

DRAW

• VINTAGE IMAGES •

THE GOOD AND THE BEAUTIFUL LIBRARY

Sample from Level Three

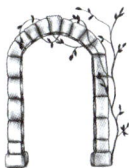

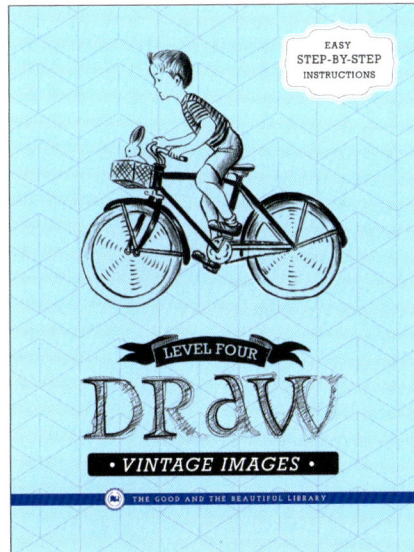

EASY STEP-BY-STEP INSTRUCTIONS

LEVEL FOUR

DRAW

• VINTAGE IMAGES •

THE GOOD AND THE BEAUTIFUL LIBRARY

Sample from Level Four

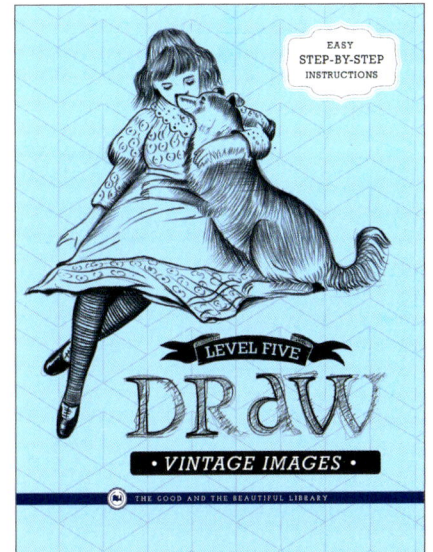

EASY STEP-BY-STEP INSTRUCTIONS

LEVEL FIVE

DRAW

• VINTAGE IMAGES •

THE GOOD AND THE BEAUTIFUL LIBRARY

Sample from Level Five

DISCOVER NEW ADVENTURES IN OUR GOLD TALES SERIES!

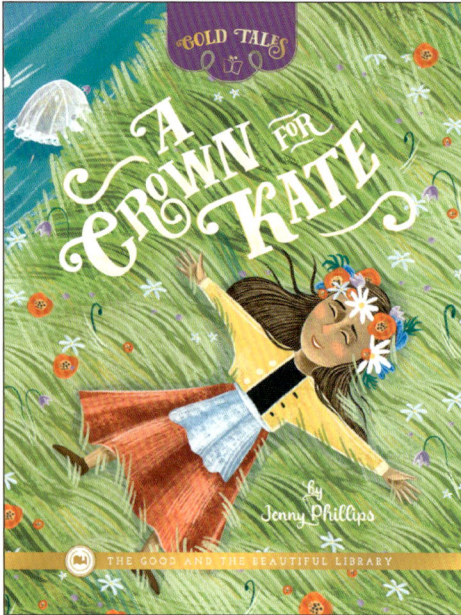

A Crown for Kate
By Jenny Phillips

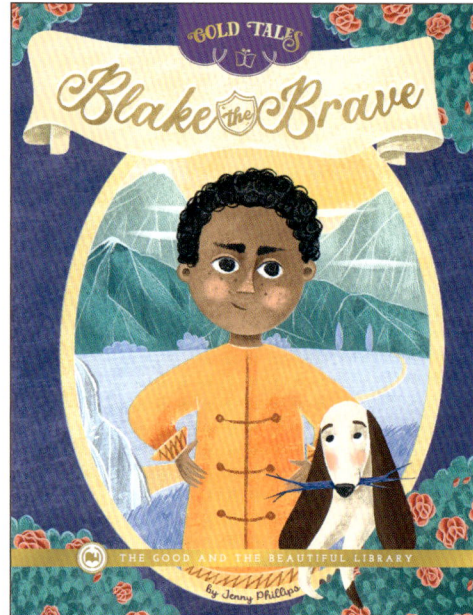

Blake the Brave
By Jenny Phillips

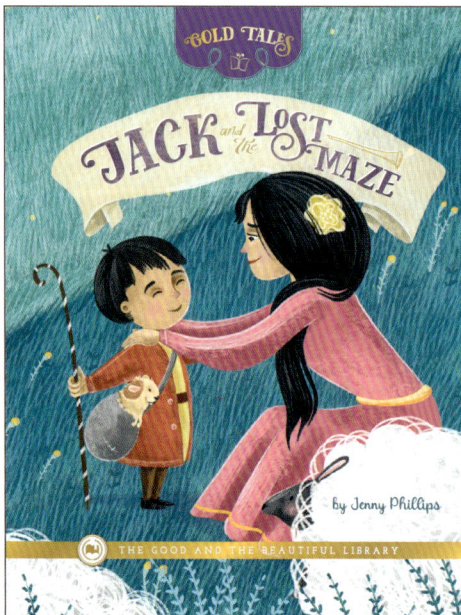

Jack and the Lost Maze
By Jenny Phillips

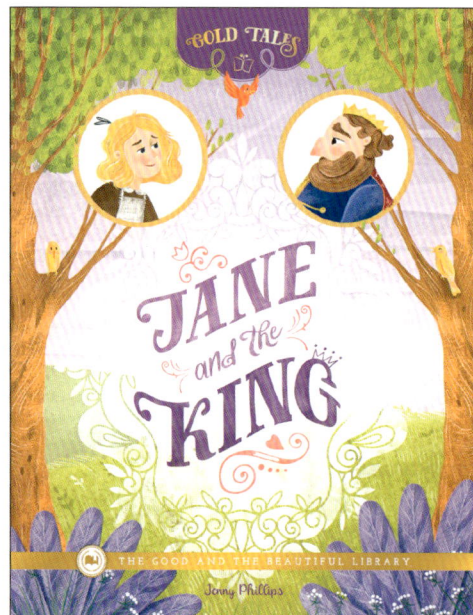

Jane and the King
By Jenny Phillips

1.0WE403 Printed in S. Korea Mar-2024